The Tao of User Experience
Robert Hoekman Jr
www.rhjr.net

© 2014 GetOnMyBike, LLC

ISBN: 978-1-304-80532-4

Notice of Rights
All rights reserved. No part of this book may be reproduced or transmitted in any form by any means, electronic, mechanical, photocopying, recording, or otherwise, without the prior written permission of the publisher. To acquire permission for reprints and excerpts, contact info@rhjr.net.

Nothing lasts in the web industry but its lessons. Nothing I have done as a User Experience professional can remain but the words I give over to those who come next.

This is for the designers, the programmers, the marketers, the CEOs, the startups, the mega-corporations. It's everything I have learned, all I wish to impart on the subject of User Experience as a profession, a goal, an idea.

It should not be one of the hundreds of things you read on your screen and then set aside. To serve its purpose, it must sit outside of your screen — in your pocket, on your desk, in your hand as you pass it on to a coworker — a tangible artifact to remind you of what User Experience is, what it means, and what it can be.

The Tao of User Experience

Robert Hoekman Jr

Just so we're clear:

A design is a plan.
To design is to plan.
A designer is a planner.

1

User Experience is the net sum of every interaction a person has with an organization, be it marketing material, a customer service call, or the product or service itself. A user's impressions are shaped by an organization's beliefs and practices as much as by the purpose and the value its products hold in his or her life.

2

The solvers of humanity's problems, the conceivers of its potential, will be those who apply their skill, talent, knowledge, and experience to design and redesign the world around us. Those who consider the way things are, the way they could be, why they are one way or another, and why (and *if*) they should be different.

"Designers" or not, the creators of the future are those who design.

3

Not all people are Designers.

All people design.

4

User Experience is strategic. It begins with an idea, and continues through every moment of the customer lifecycle, from attention to abandonment and beyond.

5

No matter how perfect your design, users will find its flaws.

No matter how thorough your plan, users will do what you did not intend.

Expect this.

6

Know this, above all else:

No matter the user's behavior, *you* made it happen.

7

Know the ways your users misinterpret your intent.

Know that, to them, it is not a misinterpretation.

8

They don't care about you. They care about themselves.

They want what they want, not what you want.

They are the same as you.

9

Revise based on what you learn.

Revise for no other reason.

10

An experience cannot be designed. It can be influenced. A designer's work is to be the influencer.

11

Human beings do not know why they do what they do. They do not know what they would do in hypothetical situations.

Observe.

It is the only way to know.

12

Don't fault them for incorrectly reporting their own behavior. You do the same.

13

The problem expressed by a user is almost never the real problem.

The real problem is almost never the first one you identify. Or the next.

Or the next.

14

Problems move from one place to the next, an effect of treating symptoms rather than diseases.

Treatment of a false problem is temporary, and shallow, and will cause new problems.

When you solve a true problem, its symptoms disappear as if they never existed.

15

One man's error is another man's insight.

16

You design pages filled with a user's content.

Also design pages devoid of it.

17

Not all users want what you want them to. This is okay. Design for those who do. Design for those who will.

18

What you want for your product is as important as what your users want out of your product. Your vision is as important as their will.

19

Your vision.

There is no success without it.

Write it. Know it. Evangelize it. Make no decision without its guidance.

Or stop now.

20

Users are only "users" when using something. Otherwise, and even then, they are people.

Treat them so.

21

Know, understand, empathize with, and treat your users as your friends. No one but your friends has more power to support your ambitions.

22

Every detail of a company and its product says something about it.

Design ensures these messages are put forth with purpose and on purpose.

23

User Experience is discovery, vision definition, strategy, planning, execution, measurement, iteration.

24

Design requires a willingness to be wrong until you are right, to explore until the best answer is found, and to question answers when they are no longer best.

25

The opposite of design is dogma.

26

Great products and services require bravery.
Design puts a shape to your courage.

27

Your design is the evidence of your thinking.

Clarity in the former is clarity in the latter.

28

The smartest person in the room is not the one who supplies the most answers, but the one who asks the most questions.

29

Great design is not the mere logical conclusion to research, but the result of a courageous belief in what you are doing, and a determination to do it well.

30

A designer's purpose is to listen, observe, understand, sympathize, empathize, synthesize, and glean insights to "make the invisible visible" (Hillman Curtis).

31

A designer's work, like a writer's, is to twist and stretch and shape a conceptualized piece of work over and over until it achieves its best form.

If it is not worth this attention, it is not worth any attention.

32

The opposite of insight is opinion.

33

Designers do not mandate, they educate.

34

The best decision is often the best guess.

Designers inform their instincts through observation, consideration, research, testing, and more so that these guesses may be right.

35

Designers enable organizations to change the world, define the future, create value, and make money. The evidence of this is endless.

36

The opposite of leadership is management.

37

No matter what you do, you're in Sales.

38

A designer's care is revealed by what is not on the page as much as by what is.

39

The less the user *must* do, the more you both gain.

Note the emphasis.

40

A user's desire is not to stay on your website. It is to *leave* your website. Design for that.

41

A significant part of design is convincing people you are right.

To do that well, you must show evidence.

To do that well, you must have evidence.

42

A hunch is not evidence.

But it is based on evidence.

43

History and psychology are significant evidence. Not every idea must be evaluated as if we have learned nothing from either.

44

Design without constraints is decoration.

45

A design is an ecosystem. Disrupt one thing and you disrupt others. A designer's work is to foresee what will be disrupted and how.

46

When a user says something is a problem, she's almost always right.

When a user prescribes a solution, he's almost always wrong.

47

To a user, a bug is a user experience problem.

It is.

48

You see the engine. They see the shell.

You see a 3D map. They see a flat line.

You see what's behind the page. They see what's on it.

You see your intention. They see your result.

You see meaning. They try to find it.

49

No matter the work, it will get under your skin.
Let it not be a cancer.

50

For determining problems with an existing design, usability testing is more expensive, more time consuming, and no more effective than individual review. For this purpose, trust a knowledgeable designer's assessment.

51

Usability testing is best for three things:

To validate and improve upon ideas.
To inform a designer's instincts.
To satiate an institutional requirement for proof.

52

There is more truth in data than in conversation.

There is more understanding in observation than in either.

53

In data, a person who is engaged looks the same as one who is paralyzed. A person who is exploratory looks the same as one who is lost.

No metric has value in isolation. It is but a piece of a larger story.

54

A designer requires trust. Use evidence to gain it.

Continue to use evidence once you have it.

55

Revise designs between usability test sessions.

Revise only what you believe should be revised.

56

To design a task flow, write the usability test plan for the task.

You'll know what to do next.

57

Create a prototype, then use it as a user would. You'll see what's missing. You'll see what's wrong.

Repeat.

58

When he believes he has thought of everything is when a designer becomes least valuable.

59

"Build until we know what to build" is the same as, "We have no vision and we're burning someone else's money."

Funding is not an excuse to wander in the dark.

60

Good designers have an encyclopedic understanding of why buttons should have text labels.

61

To draw a large audience to a training session or article, put a number in the title.

"10 Ways to Hack an Audience."

Understand what this fact says about human nature.

Know that it does not mean we are lazy or foolish.

You are not lazy or foolish. You would be won by the same tactic.

62

Make your points quotable. Attendees and readers will remember them, and share them.

63

No one attends a training session or presentation to read text on a projection screen.

Know why they do attend.

64

Stop reading design books. Start reading psychology books.

65

Adding to a UX proposal a list of artifacts to be designed is akin to agreeing to two chairs, a couch, and a fireplace before knowing the style and layout of the house.

Research, understand, synthesize, posit, validate, document, *then* list what needs to be completed.

66

Determine what is to be designed.

That is design.

67

Avoid corporate jargon. To blend in through meaningless terminology is to dilute your power.

Clarity is your message, not patter. Jargon is the language of the limp.

68

Good design comes from small steps. Important design comes from giant leaps.

69

A design is not an experience. A design is a design. An experience is an experience. To confuse these terms is to confuse your purpose.

70

"Fast, easy, and intuitive" are not design criteria. They are requirements. Do not list them in any design document. Know them intrinsically.

71

Design criteria (project-specific principles) express the objectives of a design. Write them, whether for an entire site or a single task flow. Use them to guide and vet every decision.

72

The opposite of a goal is a platitude.

In vision definition, design criteria, and success metrics:

Be specific.

73

Success metrics (project-specific statistics) tell us whether or not a decision is correct. Write them, for entire sites and single task flows. Track them. Promote them. Revise based on them.

74

"Typical users" want things to be easy, and intuitive, and fast.

So do "savvy users."

There is no difference.

They all have better things to do.

75

Don't create temporary deliverables. Create lasting guidelines.

76

Client payments are independent of designer deliverables. If you are a consultant, schedule them separately.

77

"User Experience" is weak, ineffective, and inaccurate. It is also a household name.

Semantic arguments serve no one.

Shut up and do your job.

78

Use any tool you wish. Learn when and how to use it well.

Know that it is a tool and not a superlative.

79

Question everything.

Do not question *certain* things.

Question *everything*.

Repeat.

80

To succeed, you must communicate to users through your designs and to clients through your words and actions.

Study storytellers, designers, public speakers, writers, and philosophers. Become a master.

81

You cannot design for people without understanding. You cannot understand without study.

82

Ignore what people say and consider what they do, then ignore what they do and consider why they do it.

83

Explain every design decision you make. It helps you think. It helps others understand. It gives you both the opportunity to question the decision and make a better one.

84

The difference between users is not their intelligence. It is their willingness.

They are not stupid. They are busy. They care about other things. They are experts on other subjects.

Design is an act of respect.

Designers who believe in the existence of stupid users are not designers.

85

Ask why.

Then ask again.

Do not skip this step.

86

Every detail affects the user's experience.

Not every detail is designed.

It should be.

87

Every design you see, online and off:

What is good about it?
What is bad?
Why was it done that way?
What are its effects?

Answer each question. Question each answer.

88

In the beginning:

Most of what you hear will be status quo bullshit.
Most of what you do will be a mistake.
Most of what you believe will be proven wrong.

To be a designer is to see past all this, to push beyond it.

89

The less important the task is to the user, the less tolerant he is of its obstacles, the less willing she is to persist through them.

This does not mean we should make the task easier.

Design for the common, the important. All else should remain accessible, but in the shadows.

Accept the complaints. Do not adjust for them.

90

Trends, standards, best practices, personal biases, mediocrity, outright foolishness.

They are the same.

91

Don't follow. Lead.

92

Make decisions. All the time.

93

Your job is not to do what the client wants. It is to recommend solutions and provide evidence of their merit.

Explain this first.

Do not contribute to bad decisions.

94

Design.

A lot.

It's the only way to become better.

95

All progress depends on the breaking of rules, the questioning of standards, the defying of the status quo. It is not a flight of fancy to do so. To achieve anything worth achieving, it is a moral imperative.

Seek out those who separate themselves from the pack.

Separate yourself from it as well.

96

Safe never kicks ass.

www.ingramcontent.com/pod-product-compliance
Lightning Source LLC
Chambersburg PA
CBHW070425180526
45158CB00017B/765